MORE WELCOME SPEECHES

And Emergency Addresses for All Occasions

by

HERSCHEL H. HOBBS

ZONDERVAN PUBLISHING HOUSE

OF THE ZONDERVAN CORPORATION
GRAND RAPIDS, MICHIGAN 49506

Dedicated to
FELLOWSHIP
among all men everywhere

MORE WELCOME SPEECHES
Copyright © 1968 by
Zondervan Publishing House
Grand Rapids, Michigan

Fourteenth printing January 1980
ISBN 0-310-26121-X

Printed in the United States of America

PREFACE

If you remove a glowing ember from the fire it soon dies out. Conversely if you draw a dead ember into the fire it will soon begin to glow.

The same is true of people. By nature they belong together, not in body alone but in spirit. A person can be in a crowd, and still feel left out. In every gathering, especially one including visitors, it is necessary to *break the ice* in order to produce a spirit of *togetherness*. A hearty word of welcome is most essential on such occasions.

Several years ago the author was asked to write a little book of *Welcome Speeches*. The response to this volume indicates that it met a need. Therefore, we were happy to respond to the publisher's request to write a second volume of a similar nature.

In so brief a work it is impossible to cover every possible situation. But we have sought to imagine a variety of occasions in which a word of welcome would be necessary. We trust that it will be possible to adapt these to other situations which are not specifically covered.

Primarily we have dealt with church meetings. However, certain others have been included in order to broaden the use of this work. If it serves to make one spirit to glow with a sense of fellowship with other spirits, its purpose in part will have been achieved.

HERSCHEL H. HOBBS

CONTENTS

-1-

WELCOME TO MOTHERS

MOTHER'S DAY, A DAY OF REMEMBRANCE

> Strange that we never prize the music
> Till the sweet-voiced bird has flown,
> Strange that we should slight the violets
> Till the lovely flowers are gone.
> —May Riley

We are so prone to take for granted those things which are so near and dear to us. A glorious sunrise with poetic beauty scarcely receives a prosaic nod. Babbling brooks flow merrily at our feet—unnoticed. Fields filled with food for hungry men hardly catch our view in ecstatic wonder and praise.

If prophets are not without honor save in their own countries, mothers are moreso. The unending labor of love. The midnight oil of care. The ceaseless heart of concern. Pride in our accomplishments. Sympathy in our failures. The hidden pain of our neglect. The silent fear of loneliness. The never-failing grace of forgiveness for our wounds inflicted upon them in body and spirit. These things are not for sale. But they are freely given by mothers to those whom they love.

This is the reason that makes Mother's Day one of the brightest gems in the diadem of the year. For it is on this day that we seek to atone for three hundred and sixty-four days of taking for granted the one whose life is submerged in the welfare of us—her children. On this day, therefore, we express to you in a special way the love and gratitude which have filled our hearts all the while, though often unexpressed. And knowing the crowning glory of motherhood, we know that you will beam with an unearthly joy, forgive our sins of omission, and once again fade into the background of doing that which you love best to do—serving unheralded and unsung—knowing that He who said, "Behold thy mother," does not forget.

We welcome you, our mothers, and pray God's blessings upon you this day and always!

Sidney Lanier once wrote in "The Symphony" that "music is Love in search of a word." Change one word and it is also true that "Mother is Love in search of a word." Shall we also join in the search?

Birth. Is this the word? For by it she went down into the valley of the shadow of death to give us life. But, alas, many who give birth never become mothers in the highest sense of the word. No, that is not the word.

Comfort. Is that the word? How shall we describe this word? Binding up our wounds. Kissing away a hurt or a tear. Sharing our disappointments and sorrows. Listening to our tales of woe. Giving consolation and courage in hours of need. Understanding us, when all others criticize us. Even God describes a man under His care as one whom his mother comforteth. But this is but one sparkle from the many-faceted diamond of motherhood. No, that is not the word.

Toil. Is that the word? Who can list the labors of a mother? Cooking, doing the dishes, sewing, cleaning, doing the laundry, mending torn clothes and broken toys, being an amateur doctor to a thousand hurts and ills, teaching growing minds and guiding uncertain feet, and doing a myriad of chores which defy naming. Hands worked to the bone, nerves taut from ever-demanding patience, and a body exhausted but refusing rest so long as there are unsatisfied needs of those whom she loves. But to name these things is to leave unmentioned so many others which belong to the role of the queen among women. No, this is not the word.

Prayer. Is this the word? From the "Now I lay me down to sleep" taught to her child to the supplication before the throne of grace on behalf of her household—and beyond—prayer is an integral part of motherhood. And along with it other spiritual expressions. Family Bible reading and worship. Public prayer and praise as she leads her own to become a part of the fellowship of communion with God. Whispering God's saving love in Christ into eager ears and tender hearts. Who can be a mother in truth, and yet fail in all of those things of the soul? Still there is much to be desired. No, this is not the word.

Search the dictionary through. Pore over its pages which give meaning to the language of man. But in no one word do you find that which exhausts the meaning of the Love which God has shed abroad unto us in the maternal role of the home.

So "Love" is still in search of a word. And no word is at hand, save the word which is the fairest applied to the sons and daughters of man. We spell this word M-O-T-H-E-R, and pronounce it "Mother."

So until among the tongues of men and angels a better word is found, a word which more clearly expresses our thoughts of her who means more than all the world to us—we greet you this day and do honor to the name which Love itself has coined. We salute and welcome you, our Mothers!

ON CHILDREN'S DAY

Many years ago Granville Stanley Hall wrote, "The mother's face and voice are the first conscious objects as the infant soul unfolds, and she soon comes to stand in the very place of God to her child." And William Thackery said, "Mother is the name for God in the lips and hearts of little children."

This is as it should be, yea, as God intends that it should be. In poetic beauty someone said that God could not be everywhere, so He gave us mothers. To be sure, God is everywhere. But He reveals Himself to us in terms of our understanding. And nowhere, outside of Christ Himself, does God reveal His love more clearly than through a godly mother.

And yet, it is true that such a mother does not seek to center the life of her children in herself. Beyond herself she points to Christ. Truly in the words of John the Baptist she says, "I must decrease in order that Christ may increase."

Your child is largely what he/she is today because of you. You gave him/her physical life. But more, you pointed him/her to Him who is eternal life.

And so on this Children's Day, on behalf of your children, we welcome you and salute you. And we pledge to you our best as with you we seek to lead our children to grow in wisdom, in stature, and in favor with both God and men.

PICTURES OF MOTHER

Shakespeare once wrote, "Love looks not with the eyes, but with the mind." And Coleridge adds, "My eyes make pictures, when they are shut." So today let us shut our eyes, and with our minds make pictures of the one we love, our mother.

First, there is the picture of *faith*. The faith of our mothers. Faith in God, the Father of all who come to Him in trust and commital. Faith in us who are so undeserving of her trust. Faith in the principles of righteousness which she lives and seeks to bestow in us.

Second, there is the picture of *hope*. The earnest expectation which springs up ever fresh in a mother's heart. That holy optimism which causes her to persevere when all others despair. The quality which enables her to see a silver lining behind every dark cloud. Hope—which transforms sighs into songs, which dispels darkness as it dispenses light, and which turns tragedy into triumph.

Third, there is the picture of *love*. Love which asks not what it must do but what it may do. Love which covers the multitude of our sins. Love which endures and increases despite a thousand sins committed against it. Love which at our birth was fresh with the dew of the morning. Love which in life's busy span is as warm as the racing sun. Love which at the eventide of life is as luscious ripened fruit at the harvest. Love, the abiding state of absolute loyalty to the object of its devotion.

And now let us open our eyes to see the picture that we have drawn. We see it in the person of our mothers. And unworthy though we are to receive it, we hang it in the gallery of our hearts, as on this Mother's Day we say, "Thank you, and God bless you!"

HOLY MOTHERHOOD

A mother is a mother still,
The holiest thing alive.
————Samuel Taylor Coleridge

On a Sunday just before "Mother's Day" a mother spoke to her pastor. "I hope that next Sunday you will not preach a sermon which seeks to make perfect saints out of us mothers. For I am not a saint. I am just a person with all of my faults. My children know this. And I am embarrassed before them when I am portrayed as something that I know, and they know, that I am not."

The pastor did not argue the case. For he knew her heart. And she was right. For a mother is still a woman, a human being, for all of that. But if she is not a saint in that she is free from human faults, a godly mother is "still the holiest thing alive."

"Holy" in the sense of dedication, of being set apart to the service of God. For that is what the word really means. Dedicated to God and His benign purposes. Dedicated to her children, her husband, and her home. Dedicated to the church and community. Forgetful of self in the interest of others. Unmindful of her needs in the face of those of her brood.

And so on this Mother's Day in welcome we extend our hearts and hands to you *unsaintly saints*. For

> A mother is a mother still,
> The holiest thing alive.

-2-

WELCOME TO FATHERS

The Forgotten Man

Jesus began one of His most beautiful and meaningful parables by saying, "A certain man had two sons" (Luke 15:11). The story does not even give us his name. But since he had two sons we know that he was a father.

We call this story the parable of the prodigal son. And all too often the father is forgotten as we focus our attention on this wayward, unworthy son. This within itself is a parable of life. For in life the father is almost the forgotten man. Someone facetiously has remarked that the first day of every month is Father's Day. For that is the day when the postman brings the bills to the house. And Dad is left to wrestle with these, often unnoticed and with scarcely a word of thanks.

But on this special day, Father's Day, we would rediscover the forgotten man. And we do so by noting the father in the parable.

First, he shared his wealth with his children. "And he divided unto them his living." What he had earned by toil and sweat, he gladly gave to those he loved.

Second, he followed his departing son with his love. He did not want to see him leave home. But he hid the ache in his heart. With an encouraging slap on the back he wished him well. And while he did not know the depths of sin to which his son plunged, had he known he would have shared his burden of shame.

Third, his heart yearned for his son's return. Doubtless there was not a day during his son's absence that he did not pray for him. And as time wore on, he began to watch the road for some sign of his son's return. Doubtless he was often hopeful as he saw some traveler coming in the distance. But his hopes were disappointed as a stranger went on by. However, one day the son did return. "But when he was a great way off his father saw him." This suggests his daily habit of looking with love for his son.

Fourth, he forgave him and welcomed him to his bosom. Upon his return the son showed the signs of his wasted life. But the father saw only his son who was lost but now was found.

By God's grace we have been spared the experience of the son. But we can never forget the picture of the father. And even had we fallen into the sad ways of the son, we know that we would still have been the objects of your love.

Yes, we know that the father in the parable represents God the heavenly Father. For that very reason we are all the more thankful for you. Because finitely you exhibit those qualities which we find infinitely in God. Thus we have a proper concept of God because you are who and what you are.

Therefore, with deeper meaning on this Father's Day we say, "Welcome, Dad! You may sometimes think that you are the forgotten man. But to us you are not."

HE'S SOMEBODY SPECIAL

George Ross Wells reminds us that "man is probably the only animal which even attempts to have anything to do with his half-grown young." Certainly we would not imply that you, our fathers, are mere animals. But in the tone of Mr. Wells' statement, we would say that to us you are somebody special.

The most revealing name by which we know God is that of "Father." In like manner we can ascribe no greater title to you. Indeed, our concept of God as Father is greatly colored by the picture of fatherhood which we see in you. And because by your life you have taught us to revere you, we can the better adore our heavenly Father.

As with our heavenly Father so with you, we may not always tell you that we love you or express our gratitude for who you are and what you do. But we want you to know that to us you are somebody extra special.

Your love we do not merit. But you give it to us without measure. Often we have caused you heartache. Nevertheless you are always forgiving. You deny yourself for our good, but you never complain. Your greatest joy is the joy of giving. And your supreme satisfaction is found in the achievements of us who bear your name.

So on this Father's Day we welcome you in the name of Him who taught us to pray, "Our Father." Small though this token of appreciation may be, it comes from hearts which love you, but, most of all, from hearts which are loved by you. May the Father of us all abundantly bless you with long life and happiness. And may He help us to be worthy sons and daughters that through us the world may place the garland of victory upon your brow.

A Boy and His Dad

"Between the innocence of babyhood and the dignity of manhood we find a delightful creature called a boy. Boys come in assorted sizes, weights, and colors, but all boys have the same creed: To enjoy every second of every minute of every hour of every day and to protest with noise (their only weapon) when their last minute is finished and the adult males pack them off to bed at night.

"Boys are found everywhere—on top of, underneath, inside of, climbing on, swinging from, running around, or jumping to. Mothers love them, little girls hate them, older sisters and brothers tolerate them, adults ignore them, and Heaven protects them. A boy is Truth with dirt on its face, Beauty with a cut on its finger, Wisdom with bubble gum in its hair, and the Hope of the future with a frog in its pocket.

"When you are busy, a boy is an inconsiderate, bothersome, intruding jangle of noise. When you want him to make a good impression. his brain turns to jelly or else he becomes a savage, sadistic jungle creature bent on destroying the world and himself with it.

"A boy is a composite—he has the appetite of a horse, the digestion of a sword swallower, the energy of a pocket-size atomic bomb, the curiosity of a cat, the lungs of a dictator, the imagination of a Paul Bunyan, the shyness of a violet, the audacity of a steel trap, the enthusiasm of a fire cracker, and when he makes something he has five thumbs on each hand.

"He likes ice cream, knives, saws, Christmas, comic books, the boy across the street, woods, water (in its natural habitat), large animals, Dad, trains, Saturday mornings, and fire engines. He is not much for Sunday school, company, school, books without pictures, music lessons, neckties, barbers, girls, overcoats, adults, or bedtime.

"Nobody else is so early to rise, or so late to supper. Nobody else gets so much fun out of trees, dogs, and breezes. Nobody else can cram into one pocket a rusty knife, a half-eaten apple, 3 feet of string, an empty Bull Durham sack, 2 gum drops, 6 cents, a sling shot, a chunk of unknown substance, and a genuine super-sonic code ring with a secret compartment.

"A boy is a magical creature—you can lock him out of your

12

workshop, but you can't lock him out of your heart. You can get him out of your study, but you can't get him out of your mind. Might as well give up—he is your captor, your jailer, your boss, and your master—a freckle-faced, pint-sized, cat-chasing bundle of noise. But when you come home at night with only the shattered pieces of your hopes and dreams, he can mend them like new with the two magic words—'Hi, Dad!' "*

—The New England Mutual Life Insurance Co., Boston.

So today, your day, Father's Day, we all say to you, "Hi, Dad!"

(Note: all boys say it in unison).

WHAT IS IN A NAME?

Machiavelli once said, "It is not titles that reflect honor on men, but men on their titles." When your first child was born you received the title of "father." But this within itself bestowed no honor upon you. It meant only that you had sired a child.

But today we honor you as "father" because you have brought honor to the name. And when we think of you we do not think of you as a sire. We think of you as a "father" with the highest connotation of the name. This name speaks myriads to us, your children. An acrostic on the word "father" shows what we mean.

F suggests to us the *fortitude* of your character, the *faith* in your heart, the *friendliness* of your smile, the *firmness* of your guiding hand, and the *fidelity* of your spirit.

A reminds us of your *abiding* understanding, your *answers* to our problems, your *availability* in our needs, your *advocacy* before God on our behalf, and your *aspirations* for our lives.

T speaks of your *tender* love, the *truth* which you have taught us, the *trials* and *tribulations* which we often have brought upon you, and the *trust* which you have placed in us, which has inspired us to live worthily before men and before God.

H expresses the *honor* of your name, the *honesty* of your dealings with us and with others, your *heart* of courage for the right and against the wrong, your *hope* which centers in us, and our *happy home* of which you have been so vital a part.

E denotes the *eternal* truths which you have implanted in our hearts, the *energetic* toil and *earnest* concern which you have expend-

---

*Used by permission, The New England Mutual Life Insurance Company, Boston, Mass.

ed on our behalf, the *enduring* patience with which you have taught us, and the *example* which you have been to us.

R connotes the *refuge* which you have provided against life's storms, the *renown* in which we hold you, the *righteousness* which you espouse, the *reservoir* of moral and spiritual strength which you possess, and the *reward* that we hope to be to you for a job well done.

Add all of these together and they spell "father," one of the dearest words in the language of men. And for this we honor you and thank God for you on this day, your day, Father's Day.

-3-

WELCOME ON SPECIAL DAYS

CHILDREN ON CHILDREN'S DAY

Long before Jesus was born the Roman orator Cicero asked, "What gift has Providence bestowed on man that is so dear to him as his children?" But Jesus spoke an even more wonderful thing when He said, "Suffer little children, and forbid them not, to come unto me: for of such is the kingdom of heaven" (Matthew 19:14).

Our hearts echo the words of the orator as they go out to you children in love. But we realize that the greatest expression of our love is to heed the words of our Saviour concerning you. He Himself became a little child who grew in wisdom, in stature, and in favor with God and man. And He wishes that you will do the same.

Kate Douglas Wiggins once wrote, "Every child born into the world is a new thought of God, an ever-fresh and radiant possibility." When God gave you to us in effect He said, "Take this child and rear him for me." So we are to take you as a "new thought of God" and to guide you to the full realization of your "ever-fresh and radiant possibility."

John Milton reminds us that "childhood shows the man, as morning shows the day." "Boys will be boys," we say. But we also should say, "Boys will be men." And girls will be women. What kind of man or woman you will become depends upon the kind of boy or girl that you are today.

It is for this reason that we have set aside today as "Children's Day." It reminds us of the great treasure which God has placed in you, and of our responsibility and opportunity in helping you to become the kind of children that Jesus wants you to be. It points out to you that we love you and are trying to plant in your hearts the truths of the Bible which will guide your footsteps along the road of life. It is with a prayer that you will let Jesus enter the door of your life and that you will grow up to be men and women who will bless the world that we welcome you as our honored guests on Children's Day.

We love you. We believe in you. And we thank God for you. God bless you always—and in all ways!

GRADUATES AT COMMENCEMENT TIME

"Commencement Time" is in the air. Throughout our city and nation within the next few days, young people will be graduating from high schools, colleges, and other institutions of learning. So today we extend a cordial welcome to all graduates within our church family. Furthermore, we congratulate your parents and teachers for this achievement as expressed in this milestone of your life.

I used to wonder why "Commencement" came at the close rather than at the beginning of the school year. And then I remembered that it marked the close of one phase of your life and the commencement of an even wider and more useful one.

This does not mean that you are just now beginning to live. The old chapel cliché that you are *preparing* for life is only a half-truth. For you have been living life all the while as you prepared to live it more abundantly. But there will never be a day when you should not be preparing for a greater tomorrow. In a real sense every day is youth-time to an older tomorrow.

Therefore, as you stand today upon the pinnacle of one achievement and reach toward the challenging heights of another, you will do well to remember the words of J. E. Smith, a famous English botanist who lived more than a century and a half ago. "The fairest flower in the garden of creation is a young mind, offering and unfolding itself to the influence of divine wisdom, as the heliotrophe turns its sweet blossoms to the sun."

But the apostle Paul issues to you an even greater challenge. "Brethren, I count not myself to have apprehended [shall we say 'arrived'?]: but this one thing I do, forgetting those things which are behind, and reaching forth unto those things which are before, I press toward the mark of the prize of the high calling of God in Christ Jesus" (Philippians 3:13-14).

YOUTH FOR YOUTH WEEK

This coming week in our church is designated as "Youth Week." It is a time not only to recognize our young people, but a week in which you assume places of leadership in the life of the church. Some of you have been chosen to serve as deacons, and others to fill various offices in the organizations of the church program. Therefore, to you and through you as the Youth Week pastor, we extend greetings and welcome you into greater places of leadership.

Note that I said "greater places of leadership." For you are a vital part of our church life throughout the year. However, as during the other fifty-one weeks of the year you follow the leadership of your elders, so for this week we, your elders, will follow you.

The Bible speaks of young men having visions and of old men dreaming dreams. Dreams are rooted in the past; visions point to the future. Therefore, we who are dreamers of dreams entrust ourselves and our church's life to you young people of vision.

W. R. Williams reminds us that "youth is the season of hope, enterprise, and energy, to a nation as well as an individual." You young people are the hope of our church as you give to it both enterprise and energy. A church without young people is already abiding in a state of death. But so long as our church has young people such as you are to labor with us, to enliven and encourage us, and to take our places in the unfolding future—we need have no fear for the future ministry of this church.

George Macdonald once wrote, "When we are out of sympathy with the young, then I think that our work in this world is over." This is as true of an institution as it is of a man. This week, therefore, is a reminder and a challenge. It reminds our church of the mother-lode of its future, our youth, and it challenges us to blend our hearts, minds, and spirits to the end that our church shall renew its strength for present tasks and gird its loins for future duties.

God bless you, our youth, and use you and us to His glory this week and beyond!

TEACHERS ON TEACHER APPRECIATION DAY

One day each year our church expresses the gratitude which it feels throughout the year. We call this day "Teacher Appreciation Day." So on behalf of all of us it is my privilege to welcome our Sunday school teachers to this service which centers in that expression.

The largest group of volunteer workers in the world is composed of Sunday school teachers. And no group bears so great a trust. For it is to you that we entrust not only the minds but the spirits of our men, women, and children. You more than anyone else break to them the Bread of Life. And this is especially true of our children and youth.

Tryon Edwards said, "Early instruction in truth will best keep out error. Someone has well said, 'Fill the bushel with wheat, and you may defy the devil to fill it with tares.' " And Alexander Pope gives to us that well-known couplet, " 'Tis education forms the common mind; just as the twig is bent the tree is inclined."

Yours is a labor of love, love for God and for people. Because on what other basis would you serve? For the many hours of service you receive no pay. Yet you shepherd your own little flock, your class, with a dedication which money cannot buy. You receive no wages, did I say? Not silver and gold. But you do receive a teacher's wages. To see one whom you have taught open his heart to the Lord Jesus. To see him grow in grace and knowledge of Christ. To see him develop into a fine Christian servant. These are the wages which you receive, not from your church, but from the Lord.

Sometime ago a church ordained a fine young man as a deacon. After the service a little elderly woman, with the light of heaven in her eyes, said to the pastor, "I taught him in the Junior department. It was while in my class that he became a Christian. I have watched him develop all these years. And now this!" As she walked away she was heard to say, "Thank God! Thank God!" She had received her wages from Him who promised that a faithful servant would not lose his reward.

As a teacher you are a choice servant in the hands of the Lord. The followers of Jesus were called "disciples" which means "pupils" or "learners." Jesus Himself was never called a preacher. But He was called "Teacher." Indeed, He was *The Teacher*. And you are *under-teachers* serving Him who is the Way, the Truth, and the Life.

So on this day of appreciation we express our gratitude to Him who is *The Teacher* for you, His teachers. And may He give to you strength of body, mind, and spirit as you bear the burden of responsibility placed upon you. We pledge to you our prayers, our support, and our undying love for you who render this labor of devotion to God and for us.

TEACHERS ON EDUCATION DAY

On this "Education Day" we are happy to have as honored guests a delegation of teachers from our local schools. And we welcome you with all our hearts.

Someone defined a university as Mark Hopkins on one end of a log and a student on the other end. This is a graphic way of saying that the heart of a school is not buildings and other material matters. It is teachers and pupils. And today we are privileged to honor one half of this *heart*.

More than a century ago a wise woman said, "Teachers should be held in the highest honor. They are the allies of legislators; they have agency in the prevention of crime; they aid in regulating the atmosphere, whose incessant action and pressure cause the life-blood to circulate, and to return pure and healthful to the heart of the nation."

Alexander the Great is reported as having said, "I am indebted to my father for living, but to my teacher for living well." And who was his teacher? Aristotle. Now let us hear Aristotle. "Those who educate children well are more to be honored than even their parents, for these only give them life, those the art of living well." Evidently Alexander learned his lesson well. But more than the aptness of the pupil, this demonstrates the influence of the teacher.

The American historian, Armond J. Gerson, said, "The most potent of all indirect influences in the development of our citizenry is the influence of a good teacher." More to be honored is he who teaches than he who rules. For "he that governs well, leads the blind; but he that teaches, gives him eyes."

So today we give honor where honor is most due. We thank God for you, our teachers. We pray that He will strengthen and establish you in your ministry, not only of imparting knowledge, but in the building of character.

Parents at Vacation Bible School Commencement

Jeremy Taylor once said, "Men of the noblest dispositions think themselves happiest when others share their happiness with them." If on no other basis, then on this one we of the Vacation Bible School, both children and faculty, can lay claim to having noble dispositions. For tonight we are happy to have you parents to share our happiness with us.

This is a joyous occasion indeed. For two weeks we have been busily engaged in the many activities which make up the Vacation Bible School program. Now on behalf of you parents I express your gratitude to the faculty which has worked with your children. But at the same time for them I thank you for your cooperation in making our school a success. Because the real purpose of this enterprise is to work with your children whom you have entrusted to our care. We pray that you will find that we have been true to your trust.

Already you have seen the worship period. This was not a performance for your benefit. It is the type of worship service which we have had each day during the school. Soon you will see a demonstration of some of the things which have been taught to the pupils. Following the benediction your children invite you to visit a display of the things which they have made in handwork, crafts, and the like. I am sure that you will share their pride and joy of achievement.

Therefore, we welcome you, the parents, to this Vacation Bible School commencement. Brief and sketchy though it may be, we trust that you will see in it a small token of the growth in heart, mind, spirit, and hand which your children have experienced. And it has all been to the glory of God.

STUDENTS ON EDUCATION DAY

It is fitting on this "Education Day" that we should give a special welcome to you students. For you are, in a sense, the raw material in the science of education. And in welcoming you we exhort you to make the most of your present opportunities. For what you do with these years of preparation will determine the remainder of your course of life.

Benjamin Franklin once said, "If a man empties his purse into his head, no man can take it away from him. An investment in knowledge always pays the best interest."

The answer to one question will determine the kind of education that you will acquire. And what is that question? Are you preparing to make a living or to make a life? James Truslow Adams said, "There are obviously two educations. One should teach us how to make a living and the other how to live." If you major on the former you will minor on the latter. And that is to fail in the true purpose of life.

Furthermore, you should not confuse the acquiring of knowledge with education. Most of us already know more and better than we do. It was Ruskin who reminded us that education is not simply teaching us to know what we do not know, but to behave as we do not behave.

And this points up the greatest truth of all. You should not be content merely to accumulate knowledge. You should seek to perceive that knowledge until it becomes wisdom. Wisdom is the ability to use aright the knowledge that you possess. Such is impossible unless you season your knowledge with faith. And faith involves religion. No person can be said to be truly educated without an experiential knowledge of Jesus Christ.

So as you increase your knowledge, be sure that you go on growing in grace and in the knowledge of the Lord Jesus Christ. Thus you not only will acquire the wisdom of men, but, most of all, the wisdom of God.

PARENTS ON EDUCATION DAY

In the process of education there are three personal elements: parents, children, and teachers. And they come in that order. It is parents who first give life to their children. It is they also who play the primary part in teaching them how to live. And while we do not in any sense discount the vital role of the teachers, even they are limited to the effectiveness of the parental role.

William Penn was right when he said, "Next to God, thy parents." Not only in reverence due, but in blessings received. John Locke observed that "parents wonder why the streams are bitter, when they themselves have poisoned the fountain." But conversely the streams more often are sweet because the parents have purified the fountain.

Someone has noted that Abraham Lincoln spent only one year in school under the tutelage of five different teachers. Yet he was such a man who could author the Gettysburg Address. Was this not because he had ingrained in him by birth and rearing the elements of true greatness? And in both his parents played a key role.

Lincoln's life is a commentary on the words of William Ellery Channing, written during Lincoln's lifetime but before he achieved greatness before the world. "The father and mother of an unnoticed family, who in their seclusion awaken the mind of one child to the idea and love of goodness, who awaken in him a strength of will to repel temptation, and who send him out prepared to profit by the conflicts of life, surpass in influence a Napoleon breaking the world to his sway."

Parenthood, therefore, is a great privilege as well as a great responsibility. But beyond these it is a great opportunity. What your child becomes depends upon you more than upon any other person.

Therefore, on this "Education Day" we welcome you as honored guests. We exhort you to excellence in your God-given role. And we pray for you that in your dedication to this role you may through your children bless our present world and generations yet unborn.

One of the most beautiful passages in the Bible is found in Luke 8:2-3. "And certain women, which had been healed of evil spirits and infirmities, Mary called Magdalene, out of whom went seven devils, and Joanna the wife of Chuza Herod's steward, and Susanna, and many others, which ministered unto him of their substance." One Bible scholar called this the first women's missionary society. For through the centuries women who love Jesus have been ministering to Him and His cause out of their substance.

It is fitting, therefore, that we should welcome the ladies of the Woman's Missionary Society as our special guests today. For throughout this week you will be observing a Week of Prayer for Foreign (Home, State, Local) Missions. And you will give feet to your prayers as you make a special offering for this missionary cause. As you join with other such groups throughout our denomination in this observance, you will furnish one of the greatest sources for undergirding with spiritual power and financial support the cause of missions throughout the earth (nation, state, etc.).

But this is only one phase of your missionary endeavor. In a very real sense you are the *conscience* of our church with respect to the missionary enterprise. Through study, prayer, and promotion during the year you make us all aware of our spiritual obligation to a lost world. From your program of missionary training for our youth come most of our mission volunteers. And through your sacrificial giving you challenge us to join hearts and hands with you in kingdom enterprises.

Thus with you we can sing in spirit and in truth

> O Zion, haste, thy mission high fulfilling,
> To tell to all the world that God is light;
> That He who made all nations is not willing
> One soul should perish, lost in shades of night.
>
> Give of thy sons to bear the message glorious;
> Give of thy wealth to speed them on their way;
> Pour out thy soul for them in pray'r victorious;
> And all thou spendest Jesus will repay.
>
> Publish glad tidings, tidings of peace,
> Tidings of Jesus, redemption and release.

——MARY A. THOMSON

ROYAL AMBASSADORS

(OR SIMILAR BOYS' MISSIONARY GROUP)

Today marks the beginning of Royal Ambassador Week in our church. And we are happy to welcome the various Chapters of this group to this worship service.

The Royal Ambassador work is under the leadership of our Men's Brotherhood (or other group). Its basic program is the study and practice of missionary work. Along with this are other activities such as arts and crafts, athletics, and camping. It is designed to develop our boys and young men in moral, spiritual, physical, and practical living. Its program is such as to challenge and bring out the best in every red-blooded boy in our church.

Under the capable leadership of dedicated men, this work involves weekly meetings, periodic retreats, annual conventions, and an annual encampment. Its effectiveness is seen in the large percentage of men missionary volunteers which come from the members of Royal Ambassadors.

A Royal Ambassador, as the name implies, is an ambassador of the King of kings. It is our prayer for you today and always that you will so represent Him that you may be used in bringing His Kingdom in the hearts of multitudes of people. May God bless you and use you to His glory!

MEN'S BROTHERHOOD

(LAYMEN'S GROUP)

Today is "Laymen's Day," a day on which we give special recognition to the place which men occupy in the cause of Christ. Therefore, we are happy and honored to extend our welcome to the members of the Men's Brotherhood which seeks to relate all of our men to the entire life of the church.

When God would redeem the world He became a Man. And to spread the Gospel of redemption to a waiting and needy world Jesus chose a small group of men. They were not the only witnesses for Christ. But they were entrusted with leading in and directing the work of evangelism. For divine wisdom knew that without dedicated men the cause of Christ would lack the human power necessary for the task.

I Samuel 10:26 speaks of "a band of men, whose hearts God had

23

touched." It is such men through the ages who have been used of God in gigantic spiritual enterprises. There is nothing good that God cannot do through men of like dedication.

On an executive's desk was seen this statement: "The world is still waiting to see what God can do through one man who is completely dedicated to Him." We would challenge you to be such men. And we would join with John Greenleaf Whittier as he says:

> O brother man, fold to thy heart
> thy brother!
> Where pity dwells, the peace of God
> is there;
> To worship rightly is to love each other,
> Each smile a hymn, each kindly
> deed a prayer.
>
> Follow with rev'rent steps the
> great example
> Of Him whose holy work was
> doing good;
> So shall the wide earth seem our
> Father's temple,
> Each loving life a psalm of gratitude.

GIRLS' AUXILIARY

(OR SIMILAR GIRLS' MISSIONARY GROUP)

As we begin the observance of Girls' Auxiliary Week in our church, we are happy to welcome this wonderful group as special guests in our worship service today.

The Girls Auxiliary is a part of the program of our Woman's Missionary Union (or similar group). Its purpose is the development of girls and young women in Bible and missionary knowledge and in the highest graces of Christian living. The effectiveness of this work is seen in the high percentage of missionary volunteers coming from those young women who have been so taught and trained.

Through weekly meetings, periodic retreats, annual conventions and encampments they are enabled to lift the horizons of their lives to see a world in need of Christ. Multitudes of young women have followed this broader vision to fill posts of duty throughout the earth.

One of the most vital phases of this work is the various "steps" achieved through intensive study of the Bible, the denomination, and its missionary program. The highest "step" in this progression is that of "Queen with Sceptre." Those achieving this goal are veritable "queens" in the kingdom of God. They represent the acme in noble Christian womanhood. Some of you have achieved this position. Others of you are in the process of doing so. We challenge you to press on in your purpose. And our prayer for you is that you will find and fill your places in the Christian calling, so that your lives will bless the whole world.

MILITARY PERSONNEL

During this coming week our nation will observe "Armed Forces Day." Therefore, on this Sunday preceding it we are happy to welcome into our worship service a delegation which is representative of all our military personnel.

The New Testament was written in a world that was an armed camp. Therefore, we would expect to find in it frequent references to military men. It was four soldiers who actually nailed Jesus to a cross. But they were merely carrying out the orders of their superior, Pontius Pilate. True, they gambled for Jesus' garments at the foot of the cross. But they were simply following a custom allowed them by Roman law. Repeated mention is made of centurions, commanders of one hundred soldiers. And without exception they always appear in a good light. Many Roman soldiers became followers of Christ, and became one means of spreading the Gospel.

The apostle Paul often made use of military terms to express spiritual truths. He exhorted Timothy to be a good soldier of Jesus Christ (cf. II Timothy 2:3f.). And he used the various parts of a soldier's armor to describe the qualities which should characterize a Christian's life (cf. Ephesians 6:13-17).

Some of history's greatest military men have been devout Christians. In this regard one thinks of the Duke of Wellington, George Washington, Robert E. Lee, and Stonewall Jackson. So a man can be a good military man and a good Christian at the same time. Therefore, we pray that as you are a good soldier of our country you will be a good soldier of Jesus Christ. And we pray that God may watch over you and those whom you love. May you as you keep the oath of allegiance to the nation which you serve also be true to Him of whom a Roman soldier once said, "Truly this was the Son of God" (Matthew 27:54).

-4-

WELCOME TO CHURCH OFFICERS

DEACONS

(STEWARDS, ELDERS, ETC.)

As the pastor on behalf of our church I am happy to extend a cordial welcome to the deacons of our congregation. This service is set aside for the ordination of chosen brethren to the office of deacon. It is fitting, therefore, that we should recognize all of our deacons, and that we should remind ourselves of the importance of their service in the work of the kingdom of God.

The diaconate, along with the office of pastor, is one of two ordained offices in a New Testament church. In the New Testament these offices are mentioned together. For instance, in Philippians 1:1 Paul addresses this letter to "the saints in Christ Jesus . . . with the bishops [pastors, elders] and deacons." And in I Timothy 3 he lists the qualifications of these two offices.

While the name is not used, the origin of the office of deacon is probably found in Acts 6. Certain men were chosen to assist the apostles in administering the affairs of the congregation in Jerusalem. These men were to supervise certain material matters in order to enable the apostles to give more attention to the more spiritual ministry. But that the deacons were also involved in the spiritual ministry is seen in the fact that the first Christian martyr was Stephen, a deacon, whose martyrdom was caused by his preaching the Gospel. Furthermore, Philip, another deacon, was an evangelist in Samaria and on the desert road to Gaza.

Note the qualifications prescribed for these deacons. They should be "men of honest report, full of the Holy Ghost [Spirit] and wisdom" (Acts 6:3). The word "deacon" means a servant. Jesus used the verb form for "deacon" when He said, "Even the Son of man came not to be *ministered* unto, but to *minister,* and to give his life a ransom for many" (Matthew 20:28, author's italics). Furthermore, He said, "But whosoever will be great among you, let him be your minister" or "deacon" (Matthew 20:26).

26

It is an honor to be selected as a deacon. But one should not be selected merely to honor him. It is a position of trust and service. And you are honored only as you honor the deaconship.

When the first deacons were chosen by the Jerusalem church, the account closes with these words, "And the word of God increased; and the number of the disciples multiplied in Jerusalem greatly" (Acts 6:7). When the pastor and the deacons faithfully serve together, the work of the Lord prospers.

So we welcome these new men into this relationship of service. And we join hearts and hands to the end that we shall all be used for the glory of God and the salvation of many lost souls.

Baptist Training Union Officers
(Christian Endeavor, etc.)

On behalf of the entire church family I welcome the officers of the Baptist Training Union (or other organization), one of the hardest working but least recognized groups of leaders in our church. Someone has coined a slogan, "Keep the lights burning on Sunday night." And you more than any others help to make this a reality.

But you are more than mere tenders of lights in a building. You are helping to keep burning brightly the light of truth in our hearts. Because under your guidance we gather each Sunday evening to study the Bible, theology, missions, the art of worship, how better to apply our talents in the Lord's work, and to relate our Christian faith to the broader phases of our lives.

It has been said that yours is the most difficult task in the church program on Sunday. In a society where more and more Sunday night is a prime time for television, dinner parties, and various kinds of social life, you provide for the spirtual emphasis of life. But your work extends beyond the Sunday evening hour. Uncounted hours throughout the week are spent in planning, visiting, ministering, and the shepherding of souls.

And then there are the by-products of your labors. For instance, attendance at the Sunday evening worship service is in direct proportion to attendance at the Baptist Training Union meetings. Thus you are a great force in evangelism as you help to bring men, women, and children under the singing and preaching of the Gospel.

You may often feel that yours is a thankless task. However, you know the satisfaction of accomplishment as you see those under your care grow in wisdom, in stature, and in favor with God and man. But most of all in your soul you hear the "Well done" of the Saviour as you enter into the joy of your Lord.

Sunday School Officers

The apostle Paul said, "Let all things be done decently and in order" (I Corinthians 14:40). This admonition came at the close of a discussion of the inner workings of the church as the Body of Christ. His words are suggestive of the place of organization in the work of the Lord. And an organization is built around a program and officers to administer it.

In our church this service is set apart for the installation of the officers of our Sunday school. So on behalf of the church may I extend to you a hearty welcome as our honored guests.

The Sunday school is the outreaching arm of the church. Its purpose is to enlist men, women, and children in Bible study, not only to win the lost to Christ but to develop the saved into mature, fruit-bearing Christians. What the Sunday school does will determine in large measure the ministry of every other phase of the church's work.

You can understand, therefore, how carefully you have been chosen to fill the offices which you are to discharge. In a sense you have been chosen by the church. But in a greater sense you have been chosen by the Lord through His church. For the Bible says, "Now there are diversities of gifts, but the same Lord. And there are diversities of operations, but it is the same God which worketh all in all" (I Corinthians 12:4-6).

In other words, you have been endowed with certain abilities and chosen of God to exercise them in His service. As the human body is composed of many parts, each with a specific function, so is the leadership of our Sunday school. For a body to be healthy and efficient each organ must function in a proper relationship to all other organs. Likewise it is true of the Sunday school.

In the Lord's work there are no big offices and little offices. Each is of tremendous importance. And each complements the others.

An organization such as this is like a giant pipe organ. If any pipe, no matter how small, fails to play in its turn, the result is a lack of harmony. But when every pipe responds to the touch of the organist the result is a symphony of sound to gladden the hearts of those who listen.

No matter how small your pipe in God's organ may seem to be to you, it is important to the Organist and to the desired harmony. If you fail to respond, there will be something lacking. But if when the Master Organist touches each of your keys you respond with all of your ability, the result will be a symphony of service to gladden the heart of God.

So, welcome into this service. But most of all, welcome into the ministry to which God has called you!

-5-

WELCOME TO MUSICAL GROUPS

ADULT CHOIR MEMBERS

It is with a special delight that we recognize one of the most eloquent and effective ministries of our church. We speak, of course, of its ministry in music. And at the heart of this ministry is our Sanctuary Choir. So with all our souls we extend a welcome of gratitude to you at this hour.

None of us can really know the sacrifice which you make in the hours spent in preparation to make your offering of praise unto the Lord—and for our spiritual nurture. But we see and hear the fruit of your labor of love. And for it we give thanks unto God.

In His wisdom and grace God has planted a song in your hearts and has endowed you with voices with which to give it utterance. And though most of us do not possess your talent, our souls exult in your song.

Guiseppe Mazzini has expressed in beautiful words what music means to our hearts. "Music is the harmonious voice of creation; an echo of the invisible world; one note of the divine concord which the entire universe is destined one day to sound."

Certainly there is no music to compare with that which utters praise unto God. And through your dedicated talents you strike the slumbering chords of memory to enable us to become attuned to the music of the spheres. William Shenstone, the English poet, expresses it for us. "The lines of poetry, the periods of prose, and even the texts of Scripture most frequently recollected and quoted, are those which are felt to be preeminently musical."

Someone has said that music has charms to soothe the savage breast. But your music does more. It washes away from our souls the dust and dirt of life. So that we are refreshed and renewed for the toils of the week.

Music has been called the language of the angels. It is not without meaning, therefore, that the first Christian anthem was sung by a heavenly choir of angels. Its message was "Glory to God in the highest, and on earth peace, good will toward men" (Luke 2:14). Having rendered its service this choir returned to heaven. But through such choirs as ours its message continues to ring joyously throughout the earth. And we felicitate you today in the words of one who says

> Of all the arts beneath the heaven
> That man has found or God has given,
> None draws the soul so sweet away,
> As music's melting, lilting lay;
> Slight emblem of the bliss above,
> It soothes the spirit all to love.

> ———JAMES HOGG

CHILDREN'S CHOIR MEMBERS

There is no more effective ministry in our church than the graded choir program for our children. And as we come to the end of another season of this ministry, we welcome our children's choirs to this recognition service.

This welcome would be incomplete if we did not recognize the parents of these children and those dedicated men and women who tirelessly and voluntarily give of themselves in leading this ministry to our youth. Without you it would be impossible.

But the center of our interest is upon you young people. In the words of Longfellow, "thy voice is celestial melody." Indeed, there is no sweeter music on earth than that which comes through the voices of children.

But this ministry of our church is designed to do more than merely to enable you to sing. It is for the purpose of developing your spirits. It creates in you an appreciation for great music. It enables you to express the deepest longings of your souls. Someone reminds us that "music is the fourth great material want of our nature,—first food, then raiment, then shelter, then music."

But most of all it teaches you to love. To love the highest and noblest things in life, to love one another, but, beyond all else to love God. We can well agree with Thomas Chalmers. "Music is the language of praise; and one of the most essential preparations for eternity is delight in praising God."

So as presently we hear you sing, as you present what Thomas Carlyle called "little dew-drops of celestial melody," our souls will be lifted up toward God. But most of all, it will be that through your heaven-blessed voices a little bit of heaven will come down to us. And together we shall praise Him who has planted a song in our souls.

Youth Choir Members

Someone expressed the thought that if you would let him write the songs that a nation sings, he would not care who made its laws. This was his way of expressing the tremendous influence for good which the right kind of music has upon us.

This is the reason why our church places such a great emphasis upon its music ministry for our young people. And this is why at this time we take such pleasure in welcoming our youth choir members to this service set apart to recognize the ministry which they render in music.

Someone has said that the heart of youth is reached through the senses. And in no way are these senses better expressed than through the singing of great music. It sublimates the sordid and elevates the spiritual. It captivates the highest and best and harnesses it to a noble purpose. And no young man or woman who in truth sings to the glory of God will ever bring shame upon himself, his loved ones, or his God.

Youth is naturally idealistic and altruistic. If rightly directed it will seek to scale the heights of noble purpose and to lend a helping hand along the way. Our program of music is designed to encourage our young people in self-development and in investment in the service of others.

Christianity is a singing religion. And as T. L. Cuyler once said, "The best days of the church have been its singing days." So long as our youths are taught and encouraged to sing, we need never fear that our church will be a singing church.

So to you, our young people, we express our gratitude for your devotion to duty as you sing for us and with us. And with yours we blend our voices as together we "make a joyful noise unto the God . . . [to] sing forth the honour of his name: [to] make his praise glorious" (Psalm 66:1-2).

-6-

WELCOME TO BANQUETS

ALL-SPORTS CHURCH BANQUET

It is my privilege to welcome all of you to our annual All-Sports Banquet. Some of you are active participants in the various sports which we sponsor. Others are ardent supporters as "fans"; but all of us believe in this phase of church activity.

A noted figure in the New York cafe society was asked what he did for exercise. He replied, "I get my exercise serving as a pall bearer for my friends who exercise." But, of course, he spoke facetiously.

Strictly speaking man is a spiritual being. But he has a body. The apostle Paul reminds us that the Christian's body is the temple of the Holy Spirit. So it behooves us to care for our bodies. This is the scriptural basis for our church program of recreation.

Henry Ward Beecher said, "God made the human body, and it is the most exquisite and wonderful organization which has come to us from the divine hand." Therefore, we are to keep these bodies well and strong to be used for God's glory. Joseph Hall reminds us that "our body is a well-set clock, which keeps good time, but if it be too much or indiscreetly tampered with, the alarm runs out before the hour."

There is no better way to enjoy exercising the body than through competitive sports. Therefore, our church provides for such an activity through a graded program of recreation. One does not have to be a star to participate. But one must be willing to compete with what ability he possesses, and to do so in a manner befitting a Christian. Of course, one grows in skill by using it. But more than that one develops in character. Thus our sports program is not an end unto itself. It is a means to an end—to develop the physical body and to produce the desired stamina of Christian character.

Therefore, we extend a special welcome to the coaches and players of the various teams. We congratulate you for your successful seasons. You may or may not have won all of your contests. But you have won nevertheless. For your bodies have been strengthened in the process. And your characters have been molded like unto His who said, "Be thou faithful . . . and I will give thee a crown of life" (Revelation 2:10).

COACH OF ATHLETIC TEAM

Two mothers were discussing the advisability of their sons playing football at a certain University. The school had a fine Christian man as coach. One mother was concerned about the possibility of injury to her son. The other mother said, "Well, I would be willing for my son to go through life with a bum knee just to have him under the influence of Coach___for four years." I tell this to illustrate the power for good which is inherent in the work with young people on the part of a Christian coach.

We are privileged to have such a man coaching our_____ team. And we are here tonight to honor him and to express our appreciation for him. Needless to say he serves without salary. He gives of himself out of his love for the Lord, for the church, and for young people.

Most of us see him at work only during gametime. But this is but the climax to long hours spent in planning and in practice which make possible a smooth-running team. His is a job without glamor. When he wins the team gets the credit. When they lose he must take the blame. But he goes on working, nevertheless, for the joy of doing it.

He teaches his team the proper care of their bodies, the maximum use of their abilities, the value of teamwork, and the power of a spirit of competition. He instills the spirit of fair-play, thus enabling them to win with dignity and to lose with graciousness. And all of these add up to the building of character which is the basic purpose of the program of athletics in our church. And most of all he teaches his charges to look beyond himself to the Supreme Coach, even Jesus Christ, as they play with patience the game that is set before them. And their greatest reward is to hear the "Well done" of Him who endured the cross, despised the shame, and now sits victoriously at the right hand of God.

So Coach _____ _____ we welcome you to this banquet. We express our love and gratitude for you. And we would like for you to accept this little token of our abiding appreciation.

PLAYERS ON ATHLETIC TEAM

There was a certain fifth-string quarterback who had the cleanest uniform on the squad. Only the seat of his pants was dirty, made so by sitting on the bench all season. One day in skull practice the coach gave him a problem. "The score is tied. We have the ball on the other team's one foot line. It is fourth down with just fifteen seconds left on the clock. What would you do?" The quarterback said, "I'd slide down to that end of the bench in order to see the play better."

Now you might not give this boy more than a "D" for ability. But you would certainly give him an "A" for stick-ability. A whole season without running one play. But he stayed on the squad.

This suggests the great value for a boy involved in team sports. Of course, I am not talking to any boy who sat out the entire season. But one thing you have acquired in common with him. You have learned team spirit, the ability to sacrifice yourself for the good of the whole.

G. B. Cheever once said, "As a man goes down in self, he goes up in God." And this suggests that as you have sacrificed selfish ambition for the good of the team, you have acquired principles that enable you to grow into the likeness of Him who renounced self that He might become the Saviour of all.

We have been thrilled with you in victory. But we have been proudest of you in defeat. For you have shown that you can take it on the chin like real men. But even moreso you have deported yourselves always as Christian gentlemen. As you have played the games you have worn the colors of your church. But even greater you have borne the banner of your Saviour. And you have not one time dipped it in the dust of shame.

It is, therefore, with the greatest of pride that we welcome you to this awards banquet. And now I present Coach _____ _____ who will distribute these awards.

TO MOTHERS AT MOTHER-DAUGHTER BANQUET

One can scarcely imagine an occasion more greatly blessed with joy than this, when mothers and daughters gather about the festive board to enjoy food and fellowship together. And in this delightful atmosphere it is a privilege indeed for me to speak a welcome for us daughters to our mothers.

If we possess any merit whatever a generous portion of credit is due you, our mothers. Napoleon once asked Madame Campan, "What is wanting in order that the youth of France be well educated?" "Good mothers," was the reply. The Emperor was forcibly struck with this answer. "Here," said he, "is a system in one word." It is not strange, therefore, that on another occasion he said, "Let France have good mothers, and she will have good sons." And we might add, "Good daughters also."

You gave to us life. But more than life. You taught us how to live. By your word and example you led us to Him who gives life more abundantly. E. H. Chapin reminds us of this in tones of eloquence. "No language can express the power and beauty and heroism and majesty of a mother's love. It shrinks not where man cowers, and grows stronger where man faints, and over the wastes of worldly fortune sends the radiance of its quenchless fidelity like a star in heaven."

So, you see, we have a heritage to enjoy and a responsibility to bear. It is not enough that simply with words we express our love to you. In the eloquence of our deeds we must make a garland of honor to place about your necks. Striving ever upward in the path which you have blazed for us, we would achieve the heights of womanly loveliness which is more than outward appearance. It is that beauty of soul which is the soul of true womanhood.

And we see that soul expressed in the resplendent glory which is an aura of gracefulness and loveliness adorning you, our mothers. May God bless you and keep you, and may He give to you the desires of your hearts in us, your daughters, as we grow into your likeness by the grace of our heavenly Father.

To Daughters at Mother-Daughter Banquet

It is my privilege on behalf of all of your mothers to respond to the warm and heart-touching word of welcome from you, our daughters. And I hope that it does not sound too repetitious if we also welcome you to this delightful occasion.

If there is one word which above all others describes the atmosphere of this evening that word is *love*. Someone said, "If there is anything better than to be loved, it is loving." In that sense all of us are twice blessed.

And added to our love for you is our gratitude concerning you. We are grateful for your love expressed for us. But more than that we are grateful for who and what you are. Beyond that we are grateful to God for His grace and gracefulness which He has bestowed upon you. It was Cicero who said that "whatever is graceful is virtuous, and whatever is virtuous is graceful." And we see this happy combination expressed in your lives.

I suppose that it is second-nature for mothers to give counsel to their children. So will you let me speak to your hearts in the words of John Dryden?

"Let grace and goodness be the principal lodestone of thy affections. For love which hath ends, will have an end; whereas that which is founded on true virtue, will always continue."

May your outward beauty be exceeded only by the inward loveliness of your souls. May the freshness of your youth be enhanced by the glow of your spirits. May your vivaciousness of personality be brightened by your consecration to righteousness. And may the beauty of the Lord ever be upon you as you grow into His likeness and develop in His service.

God bless you, our daughters, and keep you under the shadow of His wings. Thus you will not only be to us maidens of delight; you will truly be handmaidens of the Lord.

To Fathers at Father-Son Banquet

This is a Father-Son banquet. I suppose that to be true to the occasion I should address you as "father." But somehow that sounds so formal and cold. Therefore, will you just let me call you "Dad"? So, "Welcome Dads," to this banquet.

How shall I describe a "Dad"? One boy, denying that there is a Santa Claus, said, "There ain't no Santa Claus. It's like the devil, it's your pa." But that does not describe a "Dad" to us.

Someone said to a boy, "It is God that makes little boys good." The boy replied, "Yes, but dads help a lot too." And one man said that he learned the facts of life at the knee of his mother and across the knee of his father. Of course, you always say that it hurts you more than it hurts us. But as every boy here can say, it hurts us in a different place.

But the way that you have helped us to be good more than any other is by your example. It is said that Alexander the Great received more bravery of mind by the pattern of Achilles than by hearing the definition of fortitude. We have learned by your words, to be sure; but we have learned more and best by the way that you live. In the words of Oliver Goldsmith, you have "allured to brighter worlds and led the way."

We may not always understand you, but we trust you. A man tried to undermine a boy's faith in his dad who was a surgeon. He asked, "Do you know that your father takes people into a room, straps them to a table, makes them unconscious, and then cuts on them?" The boy replied, "Well, I don't know about all that. But I know my Dad."

So we know you, trust you, and love you. And to the whole wide world we are proud to say, "He's my Dad!"

To Sons at Father-Son Banquet

Mine is a privilege which every man here tonight would like to have. And anyone of you could do a better job at it than I can do. But you have chosen me to speak for you in response to this welcome extended to us by our sons. So on behalf of the fathers I give you greetings, all the while realizing that mere words cannot express the devotion which we have for you and our delight in you.

I could begin with that old cliché, "Lend me your ears." But rather I would say in the words of Proverbs 23:26, "My son, give me thine heart." For the Bible says that out of the heart are the issues of life.

Give us your hearts of *love*. Though we may not always deserve it, we desire it.

Give us your hearts of *understanding*. At times we may puzzle you. But I'll let you in on a secret. At times we puzzle ourselves. And yet we know that your love and understanding will cover a multitude of our mistakes.

Give us your hearts of *confidence*. Oftentimes we have learned the hard way. Experience may be the best teacher, but it is sometimes the most expensive. If in our counsel we can make your paths smoother than ours have been, that is what fathers are for.

Give us your hearts of *cooperation*. A boy may be born in a minute. But he does not become a man in a day. It is the work of a lifetime. We offer to you our help as you grow in body, mind, and spirit. Thus together we shall accomplish in you that which God wills for your lives.

Give us your hearts of *aspiration*. For we see in your visions the things that we desired but so feebly achieved. And your enthusiasm for life adds zest to ours.

The news media scream out the problems associated with a small percentage of our youth. But as we look at you we can say in the words of a former United States Senator, "As I look at my boys, I must admit that each one of them is a better boy than I was at his age."

So, boys, we give you our hearts in return for yours. And with you we join both hearts and hands as together we walk the road that leads into the future. A future that has a multitude of better tomorrows than any of our yesterdays. And it is because of the potential which resides in you, our sons, whom we salute tonight.

VISITORS AT MEN-OF-THE-CHURCH DINNER

-1-

A wise old Greek once said, "The company of just and righteous men is better than wealth and a rich estate."

It is against such a background that we welcome our guests to this monthly gathering of the men-of-the-church. There are many happy fellowships in our lives. But none exceeds that of a group of men of like mind and spirit.

Our men fill many roles in our church. The very nature of our duties takes us into many phases of church life. And every phase is important. But through this monthly fellowship we are bound together in our manifold duties. As a group we have no stated program of work which we promote. However, through this relationship we seek to undergird the entire program of our church. Whatever our specific duties may be, we are reminded that we are all a part of the whole.

Our fellowship is made richer by your presence. Therefore we extend to you the hand of friendship, knowing in the words of Proverbs 18:24 that "a man that hath friends must show himself friendly." Robert South said many years ago that "a true friend is the gift of God, and he only who made hearts can unite them." Therefore, in the name of Him who made us we welcome you as friends in the Lord.

-2-

Lord Byron once wrote, " 'Tis sweet to know there is an eye will mark our coming, and look brighter when we come."

It is in this spirit that we welcome you, our guests, to this Men-of-the-Church dinner. We have anticipated your coming with joy. And our eyes beam our delight now that you are here.

Some of the most beautiful scenes in the Gospels are those in which our Lord gathered with His friends about the festive board. He was a social person. But He did not use these occasions for social life alone. Some of His greatest teaching was done in such an atmosphere.

So we trust that His Holy Spirit will sweeten our fellowship with the knowledge of His presence. And may we learn from Him the lessons conducive to abundant living. So that when we go our separate ways men will know that we have not only been together with other men. They will know that we have been with the Lord.

-3-

It was Shakespeare who said, "Welcome ever smiles, and farewell goes out sighing."

So with smiles we welcome our guests. And it is no less a compliment that when we depart we shall utter sighs of farewell. But while we are together may we receive the enjoyment and enrichment which shall in memory brighten the paths which lead us our several ways. And may He who graces our gathering with Divine presence, give you grace through all your days.

-7-

WELCOME TO CIVIC CLUBS

PUBLIC OFFICIAL AS SPEAKER AT
CIVIC CLUB

-1-

The very nature of our club is such that we are concerned with every phase of community life. And there is no group which is closer to the heart of civic affairs than our elected officials.

Sir Richard Steele, an English essayist, many years ago said, "Zeal for the public good is the characteristic of a man of honor and a gentleman, and must take the place of pleasures, profits, and all other private gratifications." There is no man among us of whom this may be said more fittingly than of our speaker today.

Therefore, it gives me great pleasure to welcome the Honorable Mr. _____ _____, the _____ of our city. Let us give him a hand as he comes to speak to us.

-2-

Law enforcement is the responsibility of every citizen. But there are some men who are dedicated to it as a calling in their lives. Such a person is our speaker today.

A city is no safer for its citizens than the respect of all men for law and order. While most of us have this respect as a matter of principle, others must be brought to possess it out of fear for the consequences of violation. And they have this to the degree which is in direct proportion to the character and dedication of those charged with enforcing the law. Our speaker possesses these qualities. And he has gathered about him men of similar quality. So that our property, our families, and our lives are relatively safe.

Therefore, it is in gratitude and anticipation that we welcome as our speaker the Chief of our Police Department. And it is with unusual pleasure that I present to you Chief _____ _____.

41

3

The story is told of a jury composed entirely of lawyers. It was a simple case in which a verdict seemed to be possible in a very few moments. Yet the jury was behind closed doors from 10:00 A.M. until 6:00 P.M. Finally, the judge sent the bailiff to inquire if a verdict had been reached. He reported to the judge, "Verdict nothing! Why, they have not even elected a foreman yet."

We often jest about lawyers splitting the fine points of law. But, in truth, it is in the exactness of interpretation wherein lies our greatest legal safety. Someone said that "the good need fear no law; it is his safety, and the bad man's awe."

William Pitt, the great English statesman, said, "Where law ends, tyranny begins." And J. G. Holland remarked, "Laws are the very bulwarks of liberty; they define every man's rights, and defend the individual liberties of all men."

An unknown English political writer said of lawyers that "their profession is supported by the indiscriminate defense of right and wrong."

Such a lawyer is our speaker today. So it is with pleasure that I welcome him and present to you the Honorable _____ _____, the Attorney General of our State.

4

This is Fire Prevention Week. And it is our privilege to welcome as our speaker Chief _____ _____ of our City Fire Department.

There is not a one of us but who at one time or another wanted to be a fireman. But this desire was born, no doubt, from the glamor of seeing red fire engines rush through the streets with their bells ringing and their sirens sounding. Little did we know of the experience of sleeping with one eye open, awaiting the call that would send the firemen out to brave all kinds of weather and danger. However, because of such brave, dedicated men, we go about our business, and lie down to sleep at night in the knowledge that these guardians of our city are on the alert.

Perhaps we are less aware of the non-glamorous phase of our fire department's work—that of fire prevention. It is far better to be cautious than sorry. Shakespeare once wrote, "When clouds are seen wise men put on their cloaks." And more to the point, he added, "Things done well and with care, exempt themselves from fear."

Therefore we have asked our fire chief to come and tell us how we may assist him and his force to make our city safe from one of the greatest destroyers of life and property. Chief, we are in your hands.

MINISTER AS SPEAKER AT CIVIC CLUB

-1-

A certain minister moved from one pastorate to another. In his previous city he had been a member of the _____ Club. Now in his new city he was being inducted into the membership of the same club in that city. Thinking to play a joke on him the president said that he had been given the classification of "Hog Caller." After the laughter had subsided, the minister replied, "Well, I thought I was coming here to be the shepherd of the sheep. But, of course, you know your people better than I do."

We have as our speaker today the Reverend _____ _____ of the _____ _____ Church. And we welcome him with the hope that after having been with us he will feel that he has been shepherding the sheep and not calling the hogs. It is with great pleasure that I present to you the Reverend _____ _____.

-2-

One of the purposes of our club is to emphasize the support of our churches. Robert South, an English clergyman, once said, "If there were not a minister in every parish, you would quickly find cause to increase the number of constables; and if churches were not employed as places to hear God's law, there would be need of them to be prisons for law-breakers." So which shall it be for our city, more preachers or more policemen, more houses for praise or houses for prisons? The answer lies with us.

It is to strengthen us in our resolve to support our churches that we have invited one of our pastors to speak to us today. Therefore, we welcome the Reverend _____ _____, pastor of the _____ Church. Our companion in the cause of righteousness, we shall hear you with pleasure and profit.

-3-

The story is told of a lady who left the church auditorium at 12:30

one Sunday. Someone on the outside asked her, "Is the preacher through yet?" She said, "He's been through for thirty minutes. But he just won't quit."

But this was not our speaker today. He qualifies under the definition of a sermon as having something to say, standing up and saying it, and then sitting down. You will see what I mean as we welcome the Reverend Doctor ___ ___, who will now speak to us.

Newspaper Editor as Speaker

Many years ago Henry Ward Beecher said, "Newspapers are the schoolmasters of the common people—a greater treasure to them than uncounted millions of gold." More recently F. B. Sanborn added, "The careful reader of a few good newspapers can learn more in a year than most scholars do in their great libraries."

Our city is proud of its newspapers. We may not like or agree with everything in them. But they do not make news, they report it. And that which we do not like too often is a reflection of ourselves and our neighbors.

However, there is no greater force among us for the molding of public opinion. The record will show that our newspapers are at the root of every movement for the betterment of our community.

In a very real sense a newspaper is the lengthened shadow of the man who is at its helm. William Cullen Bryant was right when he wrote, "The press is good or evil according to the character of those who direct it. It is a mill that grinds all that is put into its hopper. Fill the hopper with poisoned grain and it will grind it to meal, but there is death in the bread."

But because the ___ has a man of noble character as its editor, it produces wholesome "bread" for its readers. Therefore, it is with delight that we welcome as our speaker the Honorable ___ ___, editor of the ___.

Wives of Civic Club Members

Today is Ladies Day in our ___ Club. An auxiliary to our club is the ___ Club, made up of the wives of our members. So it is with a special pride and joy that we welcome the members of the ___ Club to our meeting at this hour.

The Bible says that God first made man, and then made woman

after him. And some egotistical male remarked that she has been after him ever since. The Bible also says that Eve was made from one of Adam's ribs. Some wag notes that one night Adam came home very late. Eve did not ask him with whom he had been. But after he had fallen asleep she counted his ribs.

However, someone has drawn from the "rib" idea a more beautiful thought. When God made woman He did not take a bone from Adam's head, to indicate that she was to rule over him. Neither did He take a bone from his foot, to indicate that he was to rule over her. Rather, He took a bone from his side, from his bosom, nearest to his heart. Thus she is to be the wife of his bosom, the object of his affections, the darling of his heart. She is to stand by his side as his equal, his helpmate, sharing alike with him the joys and sorrows, victories and defeats of his life.

Therefore, as our helpmates you are the queens of our homes, the mothers of our children, and our helpers in the building of our families and our lives. In a special way as an auxiliary to our club, you join hearts and hands in the achievement of our goals and ideals.

So keep after us to make us do our duty. Count our ribs if you must, but have faith in us and love us to the end that together we may be the kind of men and women that God intends that we all shall be.

Husbands at Ladies Civic Club

Alexander Pope said, "The proper study of mankind is man." And I can assure you that we ladies are past masters in the art. For from the moment that we exchanged pigtails for curls, paperdolls for real people, and a shiny face for the beautician's art, we have majored on the study of men.

Other men have made this study with varying results. Someone said that man is an animal who cooks his food. But we know that he would rather have us to cook it for him. Another said that man is an animal that makes bargains. But every woman knows that she excels him in bargain-hunting.

Edmund Burke was somewhat pessimistic in his conclusion. "How little is man; yet, in his own mind, how great! He is lord and master of all things, yet scarce can command anything. He is given a freedom of his will; but wherefore? Was it but to torment and perplex him the more? How little avails this freedom, if the objects he is to act upon be not as much disposed to obey as he is to command!" In this last phrase could he have been thinking of us, your wives?

Similarly pessimistic was Pascal. "What a chimera is man! what a subject of contradiction! a professed judge of all things, and yet a feeble worm of the earth! the great depository and guardian of truth, and yet a mere huddle of uncertainty! the glory and scandal of the universe!"

On a more positive side is Shakespeare. "What a piece of work is man! How noble in reason! How infinite in faculties! In form and moving, how express and admirable! In action, how like an angel! In apprehension, how like a god!"

But, even so, these were but mere men studying man. Now would you hear our conclusion? Not about man as a species. But about you, a certain man, separate and apart from all other men, our husbands.

When we chose you, we did not choose you merely as a man. We chose you as a person. As a person in whom we found combined those qualities which fulfilled our ideals and dreams of what a man should be. One whom we could admire, but, more than that, could love. One to whom we could join our selves, who complemented us, and with whom we could found a home, bring into being our children, rear our families, and become a vital part of our lives and the lives of others. We chose you out of all men as the one of whose life God intended that we should be a part. We ask of you no favor but that we be permitted to stand alongside you in mutual love as your helpmate in the arena of life. That is where we are. That is where we belong. And with God's help that is where we shall find the full meaning of our lives.

It is in that spirit that we welcome you to this meeting today. It is *your day* when we express to you the love, admiration, and appreciation which we hold for you *every day*.

New Members in Civic Club

-1-

Someone has said that man is a gregarious animal. That is, he likes to associate with others of his kind. That is one reason for this club. But it is only one reason, and, perhaps, a lesser one.

We enjoy fellowship, to be sure. But we also foster many worthwhile projects. We have found that we can do them together better than separately. When we leave this meeting we shall return to our many varied pursuits of life. But while we are together we are a fellowship seeking to promote the common good of our community.

It is always a happy moment when we welcome new members into our club. You have been elected to its membership, not merely as a privilege, but as a responsibility. You will note the motto of our club. "_____." It is not just so many words. It is the guiding principle for all that we do.

You will get out of this club what you put into it. And we are sure that it will be a better club because you are a part of it.

So we welcome you into its fellowship and its work. May your life with us be enriched both by what you contribute and by what you receive.

-2-

Mr. President and Fellow Club Members, as chairman of the Membership Committee it is my pleasure to present to you Mr. John Doe as a new member in our club. He is a vital part of our business and social community, occupying the position as the _____ of the _____ Company. He comes into our club under the classification of _____.

John is presented to you upon the unanimous recommendation of our Membership Committee. He has been duly instructed as to the obligations imposed by our club upon its members, and has accepted them enthusiastically.

Our club will be a better club because he is a part of it. So I am happy to request _____, his sponsoring member, to give to him a hand of welcome into our fellowship in service.

-3-

Recently there came to our city a man to be the manager of _____ _____. In the short time that he has been here he has made a place for himself in the commercial and civic life of our community.

Before coming here he was an active member of our sister club in _____. He comes highly recommended to us by them. From what they say of him he well befits the words of one who said, "Our distinctions do not lie in the places we occupy, but in the grace and dignity with which we fill them."

Our Membership Committee has unanimously elected him to membership in our club. So I am happy to present our new member, _____. _____, welcome to the club!

47

-8-

WELCOME TO SPECIAL GROUPS

DELEGATION OF FOREIGN STUDENTS

We are privileged to have as our guests a group of students from other lands. They are in our country not only to study in our schools, but to study us in our natural habitat of life. And we welcome you in the hope that as you are enlightened in our academic institutions, you may be enriched in both mind and spirit as you live among us and observe us in our daily lives.

Our present world is one big neighborhood. Means of travel and communication have drawn us together so that isolation is impossible. Almost two thousand years ago the Roman philosopher Seneca said, "We are members of one great body, planted by nature in a mutual love, and fitted for a social life. We must consider that we were born for the good of the whole." The scientific marvels of the twentieth century have given meaning to these words that the ancient Roman could not possibly have realized. But they enhance them beyond measure to contemplate.

At approximately the same time that Seneca wrote his words concerning our mutual responsibility in the bundle of life, the apostle Paul wrote words which show how this *brotherhood* may become a reality. "But now in Christ Jesus ye who sometimes were far off are made nigh by the blood of Christ. For he is our peace, who hath made both one, and hath broken down the middle wall of partition between us" (Ephesians 2:13-14). Furthermore, he wrote, "There is neither Jew nor Greek, there is neither bond nor free, there is neither male nor female: for ye are all one in Christ Jesus" (Galatians 3:28).

Edwin Markham points us toward the goal. "The crest and crowning of all good, life's final star, is Brotherhood." And we become brothers as through Christ we become sons of God.

Your presence in our country and in this service is a blessing to us. As you learn from us, may we also learn from you. We are both enriched by the mingling of our cultures. But most of all as we touch lives and spirits. And though we shall soon be separated by time and space, may we still be joined in heart. Thus we shall achieve that oneness of spirit which is so necessary if together we are to reach "life's final star," which is God's goal for all men.

FOUR-H CLUB MEMBERS

Present today is a group of 4-H Club Members. These young people are representative of the finest in our community.

The four "H's" stand for Head, Heart, Hand, and Health. Within themselves these words speak of the aim of this movement to develop our youth in the basic and vital areas of their lives. Its goal is the abundant life of which our Saviour spoke, a life which is related to the personal and practical aspects of one's being. It is the translation of basic Christian principles into the arena of everyday experience.

Therefore, we take joy in welcoming you to this service. And we bid you God-speed in the pursuit of the high goals of your group.

BOY SCOUT TROOP

(OR BOYS' BRIGADE, etc.)

One of the many activities for youth sponsored by our church is scouting for boys and young men. And today we are happy to recognize the men and boys who participate in this worthy work.

The Boy Scouts movement began in the British Isles in 1908. Since that time it has spread to most of the civilized world. Its aim is to promote good citizenship among the rising generation. Its method is through self-expression. And it is geared to the physical, moral, and spiritual life of each individual scout. This movement crosses all lines of class, creed, race, and political persuasion. Honor is made the ideal for all of the young men.

Every boy joining the Scout movement pledges himself that on his honor he will do his best to do his duty to God and his country, to help other people at all times, to obey the scout law, and to keep himself physically strong, mentally awake, and morally straight.

Jesus was of scouting age when it was said of Him that He "increased in wisdom and stature, and in favour with God and man" (Luke 2:52). This might well be the theme of Scouting. For the Scout program is designed to do just this.

49

It is with the hope and prayer that this shall be the goal of every Scout that we welcome you to this service today.

GIRL SCOUTS

(OR PIONEER GIRLS, ETC.)

It is with unusual joy that we welcome the members of the various Girl Scout groups of our church to this service. This is a program which is open to girls ages seven to eighteen: Brownies, ages seven to ten; Girl Scouts, ages ten to fourteen; Senior Girl Scouts, ages fourteen to eighteen.

The Girl Scouts of the United States are a part of the world-wide Scout movement, corresponding to the Girl Guides of England. This organization is dedicated to the moral, spiritual, physical, and practical development of girls and young ladies. Basic in its aims is the dedication of young womanhood in the fine arts of living. This purpose is expressed in the promise made by each member. "On my honor, I will do my duty to God and my country, to help other people at all times and to obey the Girl Scout Law." This Law is a simple code setting forth standards of honesty, loyalty, kindliness, courtesy, cleanliness, and helpfulness. Its program transcends all lines of race, creed, and nationality.

It is clear, therefore, that this worthy organization is designed to develop its participants in a well-rounded program of living with one's self and with others. For this reason we congratulate you young ladies and those who work with you. May God bless you and use you to His honor and glory!

WELCOME TO A FRESHMAN CLASS

A University president remarked facetiously, "The reason why universities are called storehouses of wisdom is because the freshmen bring so much wisdom to the campus, and the seniors take so little away." While I do not wholly subscribe to these words, they do serve as a warning and a challenge.

It is my privilege to extend a hearty welcome to you on behalf of the administration, faculty, and student body of _____ University (College). I do not welcome you just to so many buildings and acres of ground. I welcome you into a fellowship and a spirit. Most of all I welcome you into a great adventure—an adventure in inquiry and learning. And I warn you, what you accomplish during the next four years will depend more upon you than upon us. We have no power to *create* a "you"; we can only help you to develop the "you" that you are.

More than ever before in your life you will be on your own. Oh, we shall not pitch you into the river and leave you helpless either to swim or to drown. We will teach you how to swim, but you must do the swimming. But there will be no one constantly standing over you to tell you when to go to bed, get up, study, go to Sunday school and church, or to do the many things that you should do. You are intelligent young men and women capable of self-discipline so as to live a well-ordered life.

In your quest after knowledge you will be exposed to many new ideas. Some of them will be true, some false. Some will be facts, others will be theories. One element of your growing maturity will be your ability to sift the wheat from the chaff. Neither cling to nor discard an idea because it is old. By the same token neither reject nor welcome an idea because it is new. Some things you know by experience to be true. Do not ever cast away such simply for the sake of the novel. This should be especially true in the realm of the spiritual. Do not be afraid of temporary doubt so long as you have a disposition to believe. But persevere through your doubts to a firmly fixed faith. There is no conflict in the realm of truth, for all truth is of God.

Most likely the pattern of life which you form while here will determine the mold of the future. If you loaf through the University, you will loaf through life. If you compromise moral principles here, you will compromise them elsewhere. Conversely if you are diligent and true to the best that is in you, you will continue to be so for the rest of your life.

So in the words of the German poet Schiller, "Keep true to the dreams of thy youth." And in the words of the American poet Hillhouse, "I would not waste my spring of youth in idle dalliance; I would plant rich seeds, to blossom in my manhood, and bear fruit when I am old." Unless the tree of your life bears blossoms in the spring, you can scarcely expect it to bear fruit in the autumn.

Four years from now the world will not ask to see your diploma. It will ask what you can do. The answer to this question you will begin writing the first day of each class; and you will add a new line each day that you are here.

So welcome to _____ University (College), to a new adventure, to new achievements, and to a broader, more effective investment of your life!

VISITORS AT CHURCH SERVICE

-1-

One of the most blessed parts of our worship service is that moment when we extend a word of welcome to our guests. You honor us by your presence. But most of all you make more meaningful the spirit of worship for us all.

Some of you are fellow-citizens of our community. And to our welcome we add our invitation that you will unite yourselves to our fellowship that you may enhance the service of our church in the community and throughout the world. Others of you are guests in our city. We pray that your presence with us will send you back to your homes strengthened in that fellowship of kindred minds which is like to that above.

Perhaps others of you are searching for that peace of mind and heart which the world cannot give. We would point you to our Saviour who alone has the words of eternal life.

But to all of you we say that we rejoice that you have not forsaken the assembling of yourselves together to worship God. Thomas Carlyle once said, "What greater calamity can fall upon a nation than the loss of worship." Or upon a person, for that matter.

Therefore, we are mutually benefitted as we join in confessing our sins, in prayer and praise, and in receiving the renewal of spirit when we bow before the God who made us.

-2-

It is my privilege on behalf of our church fellowship to welcome those who are our guests. And it is our hope and prayer that you will so enter into the fellowship of worship that you will not feel like you are a stranger, but that in kindred spirit you will feel at home with God's people here.

We have come together from varied walks of life and many places of abode. But we all have at least one thing in common. We have a need for and a will to worship. We are so constituted that we do best that which we do together. And the experience of worship is no exception.

52

So let us shut out mundane things as we draw about ourselves the curtain of reverence. Let us bow down and worship the God who has both made us and redeemed us. And when we depart to go our several ways, may the blessed tie which has bound us together for this one brief hour continue to hold us in the bonds of Christian love.

-3-

A famous English novelist said, "It seems to me as if not only the form but the soul of man was made to walk erect and look upon the stars."

This is why we are drawn together from our manifold avenues of life to gather here at this hour. Man is never greater than when he bows before God in worship. For it is then that he casts aside pride and self-reliance to recognize Him who is infinite in power, righteousness, grace, and love. Through the experience of confession and adoration a believing man's soul is washed clean and renewed. Furthermore, worship emphasizes our oneness in need and as the beneficiaries of God's mercy and providence.

Therefore, as a church family we are assembled to join in song and prayer, the reading of and meditation upon God's Word. But our "family" is blessed beyond measure because of our visitors who join with us in this heavenly experience. Thus we extend our hearts to you in welcome. May you go from us at the close of this hour with the knowledge that you have been with God's people, and that together we have experienced the presence of God.

Visitors in Sunday School

-1-

To our visitors we extend a cordial welcome. Some of you have come in response to visits made by our classes. Others have come unknown to and unbidden by us. But all of you by your presence are a blessing to us. And we are made as one in our mutual desire to be enriched by fellowship in the study of God's Word.

Timothy Dwight, an American theologian, once said, "The Bible is a window in this prison of hope, through which we look into eternity." So we invite you to join with us in gazing upon things eternal that we may the better fill our role in the duties of time.

-2-

Isn't it wonderful how the Spirit of God blends our hearts and lives

53

into one through our common desire to study the Bible? Nevertheless, though we feel as one, we *homefolks* extend a welcome to our *visitors*.

The late William Lyon Phelps, an educator of great renown, said, "I believe a knowledge of the Bible without a college course is more valuable than a college course without a Bible."

In this sense we are at the very heart of education. And we are happy beyond words to express it that you have felt led to join with us in it. We would be untrue to our deepest feeling if we did not express the hope that you will join one of our classes, and become one of us in truth in our quest after knowledge of God's Word. If you have not already found the class of your choice, we will be happy to help you to do so.

And after the Sunday school hour we also invite you to join with us in the worship service. This will make our cup of joy to overflow, and we are sure that it will also enhance the blessing which we hope to be to you.

-3-

Gregory the Great once said, "Holy Scripture is a stream of running water, where alike the elephant may swim, and the lamb walk without losing its feet." In a similar vein Charles H. Spurgeon said, "Nobody outgrows Scripture; the book widens and deepens with our years."

It is for this reason that our church provides a graded program of Bible study for the entire family. Thus as we adults are engaged in Bible study our children are also being taught God's truth in terms of their own understanding.

We are happy, therefore, to welcome you, and through you your children, as we open our minds and hearts to the wisdom of the ages, yea, the revelation of God. Furthermore, our welcome carries the wish that you and yours will cease to be visitors and will become members of our Sunday school. Come thou with us, and we will do thee good—and you will bless us also.

-4-

An important part of this portion of our Sunday school program is to welcome our guests. Some of you have brought visitors. Will you present them to us now? ——— Will those who have not been presented please stand that we may recognize your presence? ———

54

It goes without saying that in addition to Christian fellowship, our primary purpose in coming together is to study the Bible. And under the leadership of competent and dedicated teachers this study is designed to develop the Christian and to lead to Christ those who have not received Him as their Saviour.

Thomas Adams said, "The Bible is to us what the star was to the wise men; but if we spend all our time gazing upon it, observing its motions, and admiring its splendor without being led to Christ by it, the use of it will be lost to us."

Therefore, as we study the Bible, beyond each sacred page may we see the Lord in all of His glory and grace. After we have prayed to that end, we shall go to our classes.

RETURNING MISSIONARY

-1-

In Westminster Abbey are buried the great men and women of England's history. The most honored spot in the Abbey, just before the altar, is the tomb of David Livingstone, missionary to Africa. This is a grateful Empire's way of paying tribute to those who "bury" their lives in the service of God far from their native heath.

But ours is a greater privilege, as we honor such a servant of the Lord while still in the midst of life. Therefore, it is with an unusual joy that we welcome one of our missionaries who is spending a year of furlough from his/her field of labor.

Sometimes we are prone to think of missionaries as other-worldly people. However, those who know them and have seen them in their work know that they are real human beings, doing the work to which God has called them. They carry on a work much like that of our church, only they do it among people in distant lands and of a different culture than ours. The one great difference between our missionaries and ourselves is in the degree of their dedication to duty.

In truth they are front line soldiers in the army of the Lord. And while each of us has his place to fill in this spiritual conflict, theirs is one demanding a greater consecration to duty.

Most of us will never have the privilege of seeing our missionaries at work in their places of service. But we are privileged to see the needs of the world through their eyes and to feel them through the throb of their hearts.

Such an opportunity is ours at this hour. So with eager anticipation we welcome and present to you _____ _____ who will bring the message of Him who said, "Go ye therefore, and teach all nations" (Matthew 28:19).

-2-

Many years ago a seminary professor presented to the student body one who had just retired after thirty-five years of missionary service. He presented him as a "foreign missionary." As the missionary began to speak he corrected the professor, saying, "I am not a 'foreign' missionary. The only 'foreign' missionary the world has ever known was Jesus Christ, sent from heaven to earth to reveal God's saving grace to man. I am just a missionary as all of you are missionaries. My field of labor was in Europe, Africa, and the Middle East. Your fields are in Kentucky, Tennessee, North Carolina, or wherever God calls you to serve."

Both the professor and the student body were subdued. They were brought to see their own calling in a new light.

Our guest speaker at this service is one who has recently retired after many years of service in _____. I could but wish that we were as faithful in our field of service as he has been in his. But be that as it may out of the richness of his experience he comes to share with us the treasures of his heart.

And so _____ _____, with gratitude we welcome you as our honored guest today.

-3-

Many years ago an aged missionary couple, returning home to retirement after many years of service in Africa, arrived in New York on the same boat with Theodore Roosevelt, returning from a brief safari on which he had hunted wild game. The crowds wildly welcomed Mr. Roosevelt. But they gave no notice whatever to the missionary couple.

Later in their hotel room the husband complained. "We give our lives serving the people of Africa. Upon our return to our homeland we receive no welcome at all. But after only six weeks of killing wild animals, he receives this great ovation. I tell you, it isn't right."

His wife reprimanded him. She said, "I am going out for a little while. I want you to talk to the Lord about this."

Upon her return she asked if he had done so. Learning that he had, she asked, "What did the Lord say?" He replied, "The Lord told me, 'My child, you are not home yet.' "

What a welcome "home" they must have received! And what joy to hear their Master say, "Well done, thou good and faithful servant [s]: thou hast been faithful over a few things, I will make thee ruler over many things: enter thou into the joy of thy Lord" (Matthew 25:21).

Dear servant of God, _____ _____, we have not prayed for you or supported you as we should. We have so often been absorbed in our own affairs to the neglect of your needs. Please forgive us! And accept our welcome in the name of Him whom you have served and who never forgets.

MISSIONARY APPOINTEES

-1-

On Resurrection Sunday evening our Lord said, "As my Father hath sent me, even so send I you" (John 20:21). These words were spoken to a group of young men.

Down the corridors of the centuries these words continue to ring. And they have been heard and heeded by these young men and women who are our honored guests today.

Somewhere in the dim, distant past the idea arose that only second-rate people went out as missionaries. It was never true. For we know that God calls the choicest of His servants to do the most difficult of His jobs. Certainly this is true of you. For there is not a one of you but who could fill with dignity and effectiveness the most important posts here at home.

Your duties on the mission field will be varied. You will be teachers, doctors, nurses, executives, evangelists, and will fill a thousand difficult roles which can be neither anticipated nor named. But in and beyond it all you will be witnesses to the saving love and grace of God in Jesus Christ.

Soon we shall be separated from you by thousands of miles. But wherever you go and whatever you do, we want you to know that we shall be united with you in prayer and support in order that we may share in your labors. We beg your prayers for us that we shall be as dedicated to our tasks as you are to yours.

So as we blend hearts, hands, and spirits in the cause of Christ, we welcome you to this service. And now may we all join in a prayer of mutual dedication.

2

A brilliant young chest surgeon was offered fifty thousand dollars a year to serve on the staff of a large hospital in the United States. Instead he and his wife went to the mission field on an annual salary of two thousand dollars. When someone spoke of the sacrifice that he was making, he replied, "Sacrifice? I am making no sacrifice. If it were not for what the Lord had done for me, I would still be plowing with a mule in Mississippi."

Such dedication shames us all! But his is not an isolated case. For in our presence today are those who share his spirit. And we are honored to welcome to this service these young men and women who soon will leave us to man posts of missionary service throughout the earth. May God bless, keep, and use you to His glory!

3

Many years ago in England there were two brothers. Let us call them John and William Brown.

John surrendered to God's call to be a missionary in Africa. His family and friends sought to dissuade him from his purpose, saying that he would be *burying* himself in the Dark Continent. Still he persisted in his purpose.

By contrast, William said that he was entering government service in order to make a name for himself. He was complimented for his wise decision.

Years passed. Both brothers died in old age. In the record book of England corresponding to "Who's Who" in America, appeared the name of John Brown followed by a long list of accomplishments. Underneath his record appeared this brief note. "William Brown, member of Parliament; brother of John Brown."

One brother *lost* his life, and *saved* it. The other *saved* his life, and *lost* it.

I am sure that you catch the point of the story. And we are happy to welcome to this service Brother _____ _____, who like John is *losing* his life in missionary service, but who will *save* it to the glory of God.

It was such a thought that the apostle Paul had in mind when he said, "Therefore, judge nothing before the time, until the Lord come, who will bring to light the hidden things of darkness, and will make manifest the counsels of the hearts: and then shall every man have praise of God" (I Corinthians 4:5).

-9-

WELCOME TO GUEST SPEAKERS

GUEST MINISTER AT CHURCH SERVICE

-1-

In our pastor's absence we are happy to welcome as our pulpit guest the Reverend Doctor _____ _____.

It is unnecessary that I should spend time extolling his many virtues to you, for he is well known as a devout man of God. I would simply say in the words of Ralph Waldo Emerson, "Men of God have always, from time to time, walked among men, and made their commission felt in the heart and soul of the commonest hearer."

Brother _____ is no exception to this statement. He will feed our souls and challenge our wills toward a closer and more effective walk with God. So come now, Brother _____, and speak to us. We sit at your feet as hungry sheep who will be fed.

-2-

Herman Hooker, an American clergyman who died over a century ago, said, "The life of a pious minister is visible rhetoric." He might well have been speaking of our guest minister today.

Sunday by Sunday we are privileged to hear our pastor as he breaks to us the Bread of life. When he is away he always provides us the joy of hearing other great preachers. Today is no exception.

So in eager anticipation we welcome as our preacher for the day the Reverend _____ _____. Our brother in Christ will now lay on our hearts the message which God has placed on his heart.

-3-

J. G. Holland said, "Responsibility walks hand in hand with capacity and power."

These words are descriptive of our pulpit guest for this hour. In our denomination his responsibility is great. But he has "capacity" equal to his duties. His "power" is that of influence and leadership. As he supervises the work of our denomination he leads but never drives, he inspires but never demands, and he calls us to sacrificial service by his own example.

His mind is that of an executive. But his heart glows with the warmth of a pastor. For, in truth, he is a pastor called to be the shepherd of us all as we labor together in worldwide kingdom enterprises.

Therefore, we are honored and blessed as we welcome to our pulpit the Reverend Doctor _____ _____, the Executive Secretary (or other title) of our denomination.

-4-

Our church has designated the next two weeks as a period of special evangelistic endeavor. As our guest evangelist we are happy to have Brother _____ _____.

The Bible says that some men are called to be evangelists. And he is such a person. Wherever he goes the blessings of God attend his ministry, as we are sure that the case will be here.

Brother _____ is a man who knows and believes the Bible. He believes that the Gospel is the power of God unto salvation to everyone who believes its message. He has a love for the souls of men. And he preaches the Gospel in the power of the Holy Spirit.

He does not come to bring us a revival. He comes to lead us in experiencing a revival. Revival does not relate to the world outside the church. We are the ones who must be revived. And if we are, we will go into the world to tell the good news of salvation to the lost.

So, Brother _____, we pledge to you our prayers, time, talents, and efforts as we follow your leadership in the days before us. We welcome you to our church and hearts. And may the power of God's Holy Spirit be upon you as you come to preach to us.

Guest Speaker at a Stewardship Banquet

-1-

Annually we gather in an occasion like this in final preparation for our Every Member Canvass as we set our minds and hearts to the challenge of underwriting our church budget for the coming year. For such occasions we invite as our speaker one who can both instruct and inspire us toward a greater faithfulness in stewardship.

This year we are privileged to have as our speaker an outstanding business man. By both knowledge and practice he is eminently qualified. For he is not only a Bible student and an able speaker. He is known as one who holds in trust that which God has given to him. He lives by the admonition of the apostle Paul that "it is required in stewards, that a man be found faithful" (I Corinthians 4:2).

Therefore, we are happy to welcome as our speaker Brother _____ ——. We are in your hands as you come to bring us the message which God has laid on your heart.

-2-

As our speaker for this annual Stewardship Banquet we are happy to welcome the Reverend _____.

Many years ago another minister, Charles Simmons, said, "As to all that we have and are, we are but stewards of the Most High God. On our possessions, on our time, and talents, and influence, and property, He has written, 'Occupy for me, till I shall come.' To obey His instructions and serve Him faithfully, is the true test of obedience and discipleship."

That this thought characterizes the preaching and teaching ministry of our speaker is attested by the record in stewardship made by his own people.

It is unnecessary that I should introduce our speaker to our church family. For he is well known to you. So I take great pleasure in presenting him to you. Brother _____, you will bless our hearts as you challenge our minds and wills. We shall pray for you as you speak to us.

-3-

More than a century ago an American clergyman, I. S. Spencer, said, "It is a dark sign when the owner is seen to be growing poor, and his steward is found to be growing rich." How fitting are these words in times like these, a time when prosperity abounds, yet when the Lord's work goes lacking.

It is well, therefore, that we shall hear our speaker tonight with open ears and hearts. For he has come to speak to us, the stewards, on behalf of God, the owner.

Brother _____ _____, we welcome you to this hour, and we wait before you expectantly as you come to challenge us. God bless you and use you, is our prayer.

-10-

WELCOME TO NEW CHURCH MEMBERS

NEW CHRISTIANS

-1-

One of the holiest moments in the life of a family is when a baby is born. But the sanctity of this moment is even greater. For a soul has been born from above into the family of God. We welcome you, therefore, into this Christian relationship, and, after baptism, into the full fellowship of the church.

It is fitting that Jesus spoke of His followers as little children and disciples or pupils. For both terms suggest growth and development in your Christian life. Our church family wants to help you to become a mature, effective servant of Christ. Therefore, we pledge to you our prayers, labors, and guidance as you develop more and more into the likeness of our Lord.

And may you "grow in grace, and in the knowledge of our Lord and Saviour Jesus Christ" (II Peter 3:18).

-2-

A man eighty-five years old gave his heart to Christ. The next day, when asked how old he was, he replied, "I am one day old. For I did not really begin to live until I became a Christian."

Jesus said, "I am come that they might have life, and that they might have it more abundantly" (John 10:10).

Our hearts rejoice that this dear man/woman has come professing his/her faith in Christ as Saviour. And we welcome you into the joy that can come only to those who have done so. Because you have believed in Him, you have eternal life. It is your present possession not just a future hope.

Someone asked Charles H. Spurgeon, the great English preacher, how he knew that he was saved. He replied, "My Saviour promised to save me if I would trust in Him. I have done so. A gentleman keeps his word. And my Saviour is a gentleman."

Your salvation depends upon Him, not upon yourself. You are saved by grace through faith apart from any work or merit of your own. But as a saved person you will bear the fruit of good works, not for your salvation but for His glory.

We pledge to you our fellowship in the Christian life that together we shall serve the Lord.

-3-

Human language fails us when we try to express the glory of the salvation which we have in Jesus Christ. But in simple words we would express our delight that you have received it through faith in Him.

The Lord both saves us and preserves us in that salvation. Many scriptures could be cited to this effect. But none is more expressive than Ephesians 1:13-14. Paul speaks of those who have believed in Christ, "in whom also after that ye believed, ye were sealed with that Holy Spirit of promise, which is the earnest of our inheritance until the redemption of the purchased possession."

Thus the Holy Spirit who indwells you as a Christian is God's seal of ownership. Furthermore, He is God's "earnest" money or guarantee that He will keep His agreement to save completely all who come to Him through faith in His Son.

So we are happy to welcome you into this blessed assurance. The Lord will never fail you, and we pray that by His grace you will never fail Him.

NEW MEMBERS BY TRANSFER

You have crowned this service by presenting yourselves for membership in our church upon the promise of a letter from a sister church. Therefore, we welcome you as you come to be one of us.

In truth we welcome you not into a membership, but into a *fellowship*. Someone has defined "fellowship" as two fellows in the same ship. And this is not far from the New Testament meaning of the word. It means to have all things in common, to share both the privileges and the responsibilities inherent in the relationship. This is made possible as the Holy Spirit fuses us together in one spirit of love and service. As we submit ourselves to Him we shall know the

63

heavenly relationship enjoyed only by those who belong to God.

I have spoken these words of welcome on behalf of all of us. After the benediction our people will express this welcome for themselves. And that will be fellowship indeed.

VARIOUS NEW MEMBERS

There are many facets to a worship service: prayer, praise, reading God's Word, preaching, and pleading toward Christian faith and duty. But no service would be complete without this climactic moment when we welcome new people into our fellowship. Since this is so vital a part of our service we should no more move with undue haste than we should pray short prayers or sing only one verse of a hymn in order to beat the clock with the benediction.

Here we have _____ _____ who comes on profession of faith. We welcome you in this blessed experience in Christ. (Call each name and have each one stand with the pastor as he is received.) And now we have Brother and Mrs. _____ and their children coming by letter from a sister church. We are so happy that you have chosen us as your spiritual home in our city.

Well, who do we have here? Brother and Mrs. _____, former members of our church, who have returned to our city. Welcome home! Because you have been active members of our sister church in _____, you will be better members here again.

So to all of you we say, "Welcome!" God bless you and us as we enjoy that fellowship of kindred minds, which is like to that above.

NEW MEMBERS OF CHURCH STAFF AND FAMILY

It is always a blessed moment when we welcome new members into our church family. But there is an added joy in welcoming Brother _____ _____ and his family, for he has come to join our church staff as Minister of Religious Education (Music, etc.).

Our church has sought to follow God's leadership in securing such a co-laborer. And we are certain that we have found His man.

We have not called you to work for us but with us. We do not ask you to do our work, but to lead us as we serve the Lord. And while you will be a member of our church staff, we have gained additional workers in your family. We would not seek to impose upon them in asking of them more than we are willing to do ourselves.

As we welcome you and your family we would do so in the words of the apostle Paul. "For we are labourers together with God."